The Tom Anderson

C O L L E C T I O N

VOLUME THREE

From

The Shetland Musical Heritage Trust

THE HARDIE PRESS

ALBA | CHRUTHACHAIL

The publisher acknowledges
support from Creative Scotland towards the
publication of this volume

ISBN 978 0 946868 38 4
ISMN M-708090-07-6

First published in Great Britain 2013 by The Hardie Press
108 Harlawhill Gardens, Prestonpans EH32 9JH

Printed in Great Britain by David Macdonald Limited, Edinburgh

The cover illustration is reproduced from a photograph by John Coutts, Lerwick
of Braewick, Cliffs and Drongs.

Contents

PAGE

Foreword by Charles Simpson   iv

Introduction by the Shetland Musical Heritage Trust   1

Slow Airs

Avensgarth	2
Clyde Valley	2
Flangafield	3
Lunna Holm	3
Miss Susan McArthur BEM	4
Mr Bill Paterson	4
Pund Head	5
The Croft of Feal	5
Da Auld Resting Chair	6
Daybrak	6

Marches

Capt. Iain Peterson	7
Hillswick Wedding	8
Miss Chris Moffat	9
Da Auld Crü	10
Dayset	10
Ronnie Cooper	11
Sands of Braewick	11
Stenabreck	12
The Haa	12
Heckie o' da Hulters	13
Airthrey Castle	13

Reels

Angela Hughson's Reel	14
Backafield	14
Billy's Tune	15
Curly Jamieson	15
Da Blacksmith	16
Da Craig Saet	16
Da Holes o' Scraada	17
Elaine's Reel	17
Gavin Marwick	18
Heads of Tingon	18
Hoohivdi	19
Houlma Sound	19
Maggie's Reel	20
Mike Bacchus Reel	20
Miss Lisa Drever	21
Peerie Twa	21
Pottinger's Reel	22
Robertson's Reel	22
Schiffman's Reel	23
The Leons	23

The Villians of Hamnavoe	24
Da Wind ida Claes Line	24
Da Laird o' Gulberwick	25
Debbie's Reel	25
Saxavord	26
Noup of Noss	26
Da Rod ta Houll	27

Jigs

Da Cannon	27
Garderhouse Voe	28
Mavis Grind	28
The Fairy Fiddler (Ruth)	29

Twosteps

Miss Claire White	29
Islesburgh House	30

Waltzes

Hairst Blinks	31
Miss Jacqueline Young	31
Southern Moon	32
Wilma's Waltz	32
Northern Lights	33
Gossabrough Waltz	33
Mid-Yell School Waltz	34
Uyeasoond Bairns	34

Slow Strathspey & Reel Medleys

Mr Bill Hardie & Mr John Junner	35
Laura Malcolmson of Cunningsburgh	36

Strathspeys

Jim Hunter	36
Ness of Braewick	37
John Fraser of Papa	37
Spey Cottage	38
Twart Dykes	38

Hornpipes

Kirstie's Hornpipe	39
Rosa's Hornpipe	39
Skeld Voe Hornpipe	40
Da Mill Lochs of Ockran	40
Da Hame Farers	41
Da Sixereen	41

Notes on the Music	42

TOM ANDERSON 1910 - 1991

Foreword by Charles Simpson

Dr Tom Anderson MBE died in 1991, five weeks after his 81st birthday. Tom – Tammy as Shetland knew him – was unique in his field: fiddler, composer, collector, teacher, saver of tradition. It's safe to say nobody else came anywhere near matching his activities and achievements, and those proved to be a dominant influence on the Shetland musical scene after 1945. His determination established the traditional fiddle tuition that has produced young fiddlers by the hundred, and his inspiration was the catalyst that created our famous Folk Festival and a host of similar musical events. Tammy laid the foundations upon which the current success of Shetland's music is built, and which produced for our community a worldwide reputation for its thriving musical tradition, second to none.

In 2010, Shetland commemorated the centenary of Tammy Anderson's birth in Eshaness. To his pupils and the people who knew Tammy as a friend or a fellow-musician, it's sobering to realise that today, almost one person in three of our island's current population has been born since his death, and has no personal memory of the man – once met, never forgotten! His name nevertheless lives on among them, through his tunes, wherever young traditional musicians gather to learn, to play together or to compete. An older, wider circle of admirers venerates his memory, quite simply for his lifetime's achievements.

I first came to know Tammy Anderson in the mid-1970s when our mutual friend Peter Leith dragged me along to perform at social evenings in the RAFA club in Lerwick. Having served in the RAF, Tammy was an active member and a regular performer on these occasions, accompanied on piano by Marjory Smith. With their encouragement I later took myself and my newly acquired fiddle to the back row of Fiddlers' practices in St Olaf's Hall every Wednesday night, sessions of learning for the novices, pure musical fun for young and old alike; along with many others, I was soon hooked for life.

Tammy was a very busy man. His leadership of the Shetland Fiddlers' Society was charismatic and inspirational, as was the tutoring of his pupils through his position as Shetland's first schools' traditional fiddle tutor – which involved a lot of travelling. In addition he still took private pupils. All this he undertook with complete commitment and astounding energy for a man in his sixties. Tammy was in a hurry, you see; for thirty years he had recorded and collected the old music – now he had a mission to rebuild and restore Shetland's fiddle tradition, and time was of the essence. Through the 1980s his Young Heritage fiddlers, his Stirling University Summer Schools, his recordings and publications all achieved the results he sought.

Amidst all this invariably hectic activity, Tammy still found time to compose tunes. Melodies just came to him, he used to say; indeed, they came throughout his life. Looking at the dates of his compositions, it seems the more Tammy is playing, the more the tunes emerge. There's a burst in the late 1930s, when he's playing in Davie Robertson's band. After a wartime pause, there's a surge of compositions when he's leading the Islesburgh Band. Formation of the Fiddlers' Society brings another spate of new tunes in the 1960s, many dedicated to its members, his immediate friends and family, and others inspired by his Eshaness homeland. In the 1980s they came steadily and in increasing numbers, written for pupils, friends, places, memories. The well never completely dried up, for Tammy's last known composition is dated July 1988.

Tammy composed good tunes. Many – his slow airs especially – are absolute gems, renowned wherever in the world the fiddle is played, and recorded time and again by solo fiddlers and bands. With the publication of this book, his whole collection is completely in the public domain. We can now appreciate fully all the works of a composer who, if he had never achieved anything else in the field of traditional fiddling, would have been famous for his tunes alone.

Shetland Musical Heritage Trust

The Trust has as its wider aim the preservation and development of all aspects of the musical heritage of the Shetland Islands. The trustees are proud to present this book, the third and final volume of the Tom Anderson Collection. Violet Tulloch was appointed chief advisor on his unpublished music by Dr Anderson himself; this work, carried out under her supervision, completes the task she and her fellow trustees willingly undertook in 1991.

Thirty years have gone by since Tom first envisaged the formation of a Heritage Trust in order to perpetuate his activities and aspirations. Over the 28 years since the Trust's creation, its aims have been carried forward and supported by a succession of trustees, while the current financial assets of the Trust originate from, and are augmented by, the royalties earned on Dr Anderson's compositions. The present trustees acknowledge with gratitude the contribution of those who served in former years, and in addition their fellow trustees record here their particular appreciation of the immense task undertaken by Judith Nicolson and Violet Tulloch in transcribing and chording over 200 tunes from original handwritten manuscripts.

The publication of Volume Three represents a very significant milestone in the Trust's history, allowing it now to consider fresh projects in furtherance of Dr Anderson's vision.

Avensgarth

Slow Air

Tom Anderson

Clyde Valley

Slow Air

Tom Anderson

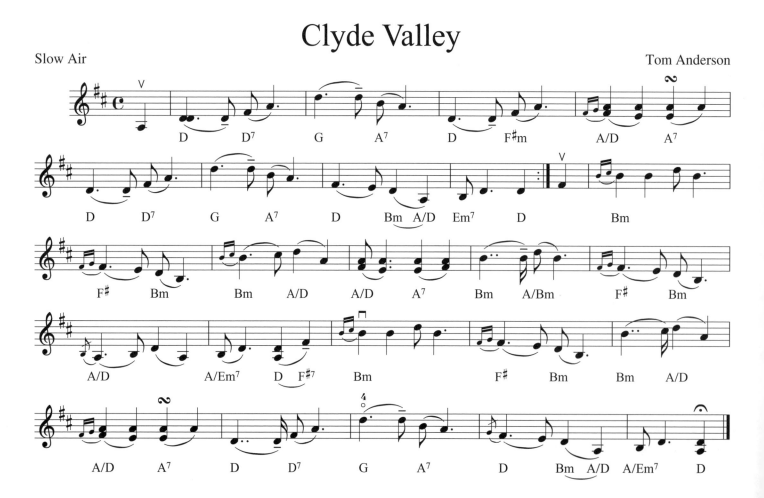

HP 31.13

Flangafield

Slow Air

Tom Anderson

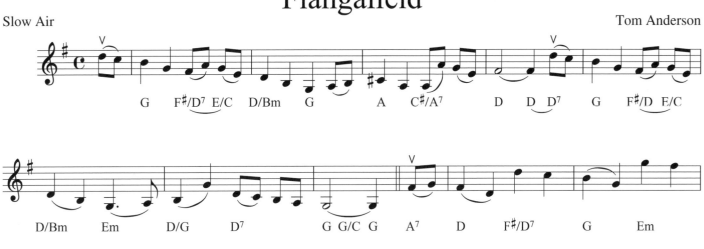

G F#/D⁷ E/C D/Bm G A C#/A⁷ D D D⁷ G F#/D E/C

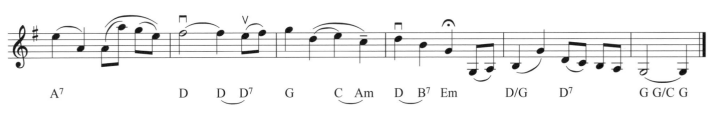

D/Bm Em D/G D⁷ G G/C G A⁷ D F#/D⁷ G Em

A⁷ D D D⁷ G C Am D B⁷ Em D/G D⁷ G G/C G

Lunna Holm

Slow Air

Tom Anderson

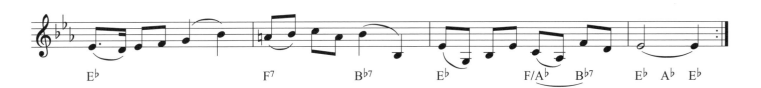

E♭ F⁷ B♭⁷ E♭ Cm Fm B♭⁷

E♭ F⁷ B♭⁷ E♭ F/A♭ B♭⁷ E♭ A♭ E♭

E♭ Gm A♭ Gm F/A♭ G/E♭ A/F⁷ Fm B♭

E♭ Gm A♭ A° B♭/E♭ Cm Fm B♭ Gm Cm Fm B♭⁷ E♭

HP 31.13

4

Miss Susan McArthur BEM

Slow Air

Tom Anderson

Mr Bill Paterson

Slow Air

Tom Anderson

HP 31.13

Pund Head

Slow Air

Tom Anderson

The Croft of Feal

Slow Air

Tom Anderson

6

Da Auld Resting Chair

Slow Air

Tom Anderson

Daybrak

Slow Air

Tom Anderson

HP 31.13

Capt. Iain Peterson

March

Tom Anderson

Hillswick Wedding

March

Tom Anderson

Miss Chris Moffat

March

Tom Anderson

Da Auld Crü

March

Tom Anderson

Dayset

March

Tom Anderson

HP 31.13

Ronnie Cooper

March

Tom Anderson

Sands of Braewick

March

Tom Anderson

12

Stenabreck

March

Tom Anderson

The Haa

March

Tom Anderson

HP 31.13

Heckie o' da Hulters

March

Tom Anderson

Airthrey Castle

March

Tom Anderson

14

Angela Hughson's Reel

Reel

Tom Anderson

Backafield

Reel

Tom Anderson

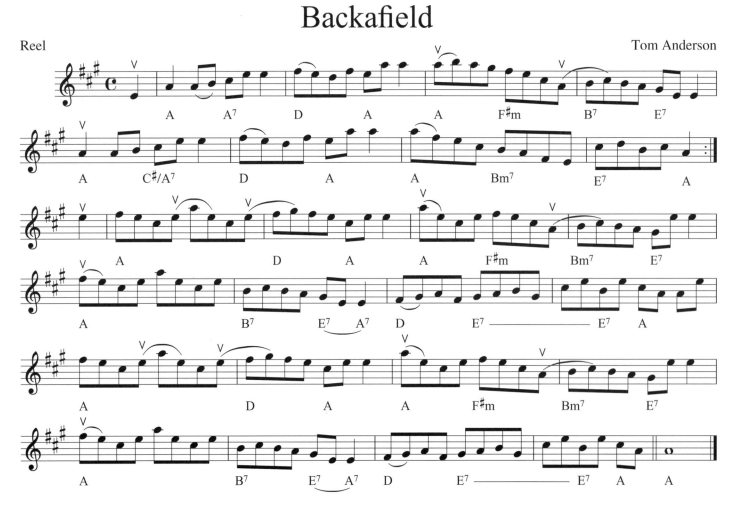

HP 31.13

Billy's Tune

Reel

Tom Anderson

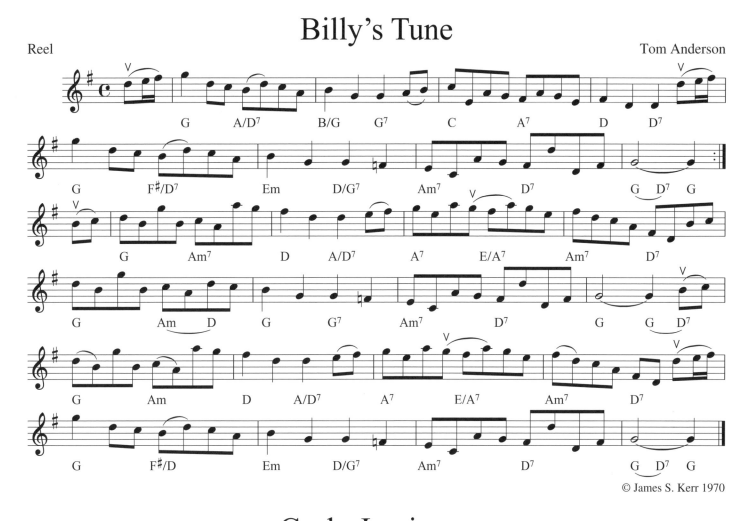

© James S. Kerr 1970

Curly Jamieson

Slow Reel

Tom Anderson

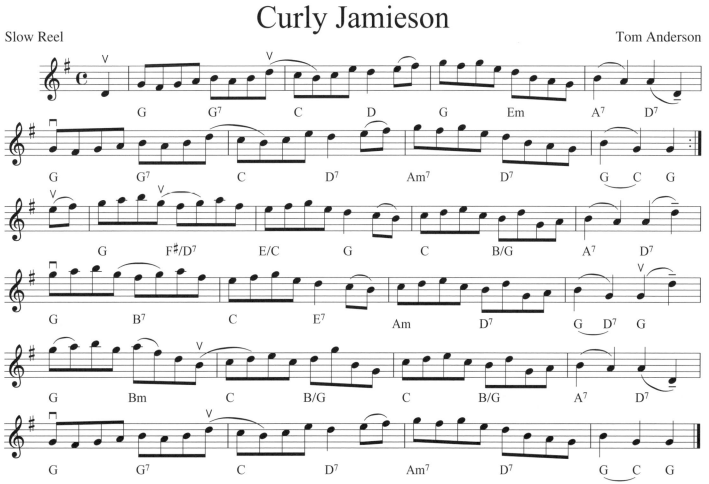

Da Blacksmith

Reel

Tom Anderson

© James S. Kerr 1970

Da Craig Saet

Reel

Tom Anderson

HP 31.13

Da Holes o' Scraada

Reel

Tom Anderson

Elaine's Reel

Reel

Tom Anderson

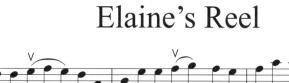

HP 31.13

Gavin Marwick

Reel

Tom Anderson

Heads of Tingon

Slow Reel

Tom Anderson

HP 31.13

Hoohivdi

Reel

Tom Anderson

Houlma Sound

Reel

Tom Anderson

Maggie's Reel

Reel

Tom Anderson

© James S. Kerr 1970

Mike Bacchus Reel

Reel

Tom Anderson

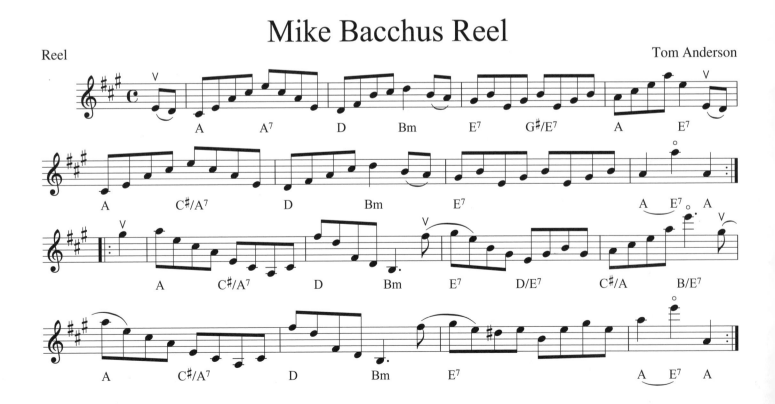

Miss Lisa Drever

Reel

Tom Anderson

Peerie Twa

Reel

Tom Anderson

HP 31.13

Pottinger's Reel

Reel

Tom Anderson

Robertson's Reel

Reel

Tom Anderson

HP 31.13

Schiffman's Reel

Reel

Tom Anderson

The Leons

Reel

Tom Anderson

The Villians of Hamnavoe

Reel

Tom Anderson

Da Wind ida Claes Line

Reel

Tom Anderson

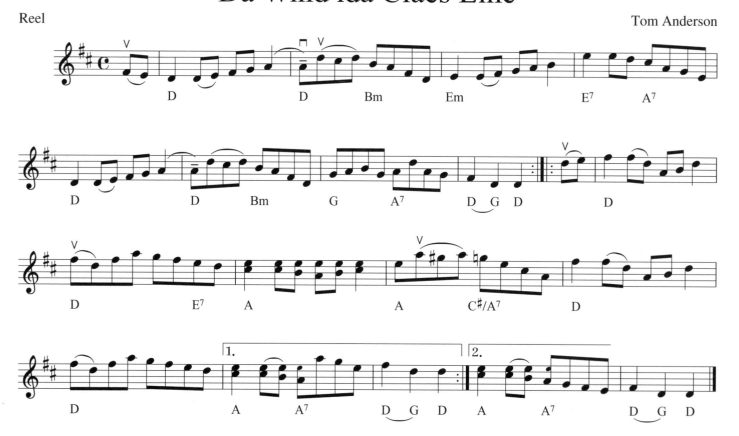

HP 31.13

Da Laird o' Gulberwick

Reel

Tom Anderson

Debbie's Reel

Reel

Tom Anderson

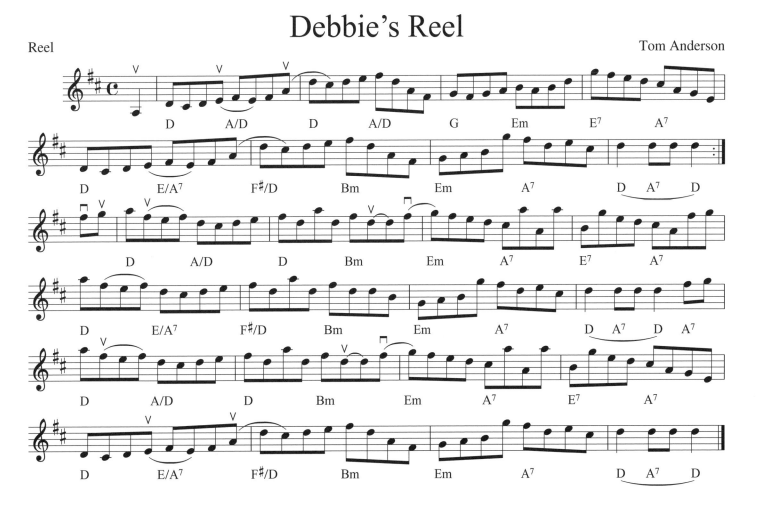

26

Saxavord

Slow Reel

Tom Anderson

Noup of Noss

Reel

Tom Anderson

HP 31.13

Da Rod ta Houll

Reel

Tom Anderson

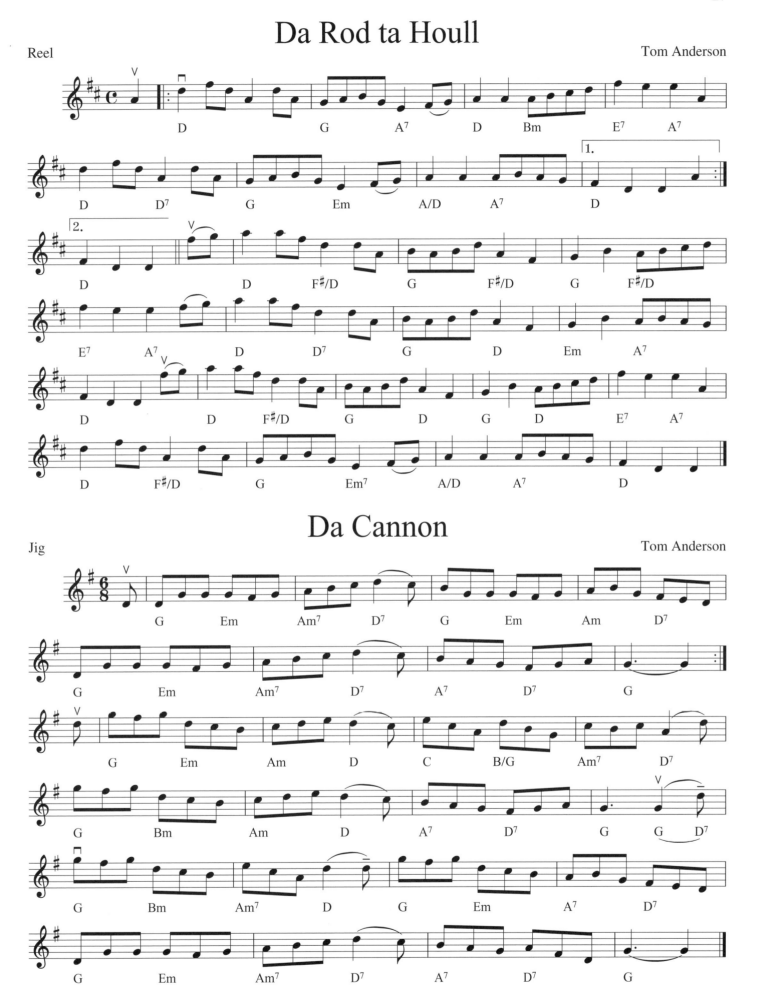

Da Cannon

Jig

Tom Anderson

Garderhouse Voe

Jig

Tom Anderson

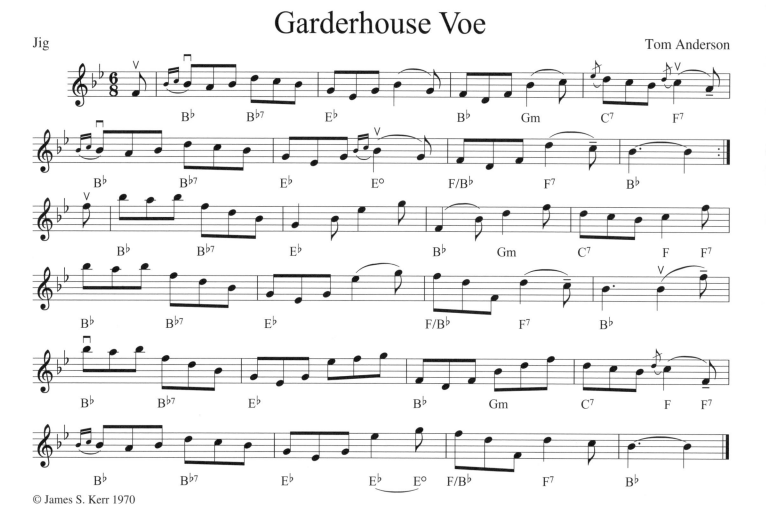

Mavis Grind

Jig

Tom Anderson

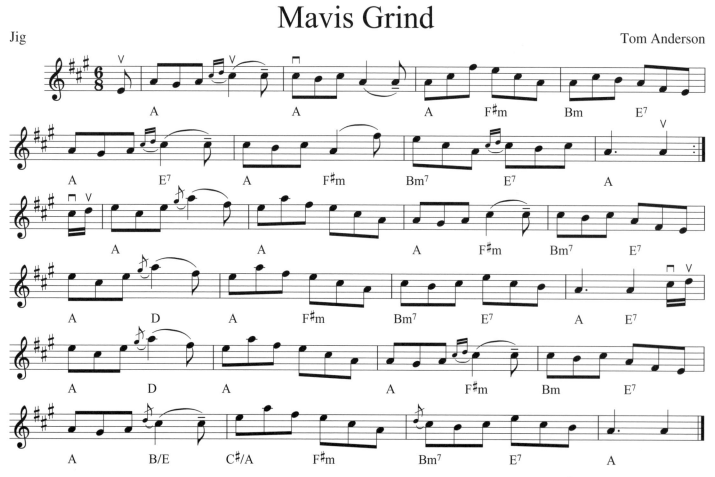

HP 31.13

The Fairy Fiddler (Ruth)

Clog (or Jig)

Tom Anderson

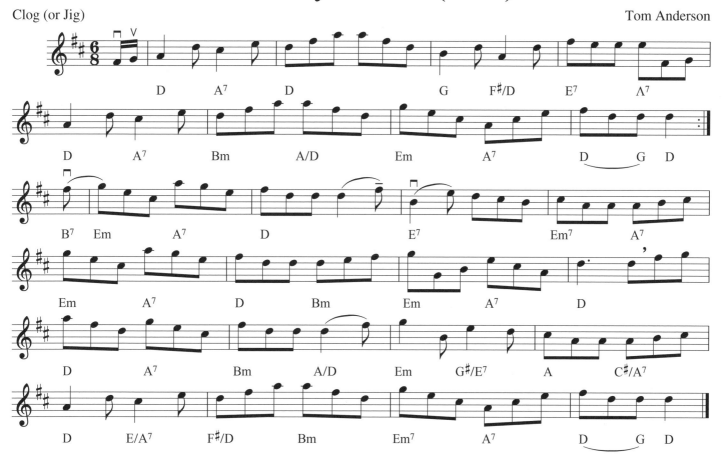

Miss Claire White

Twostep

Tom Anderson

Islesburgh House

Twostep

Tom Anderson

Hairst Blinks

Waltz

Tom Anderson

Miss Jacqueline Young

Waltz

Tom Anderson

Southern Moon

Waltz

Tom Anderson

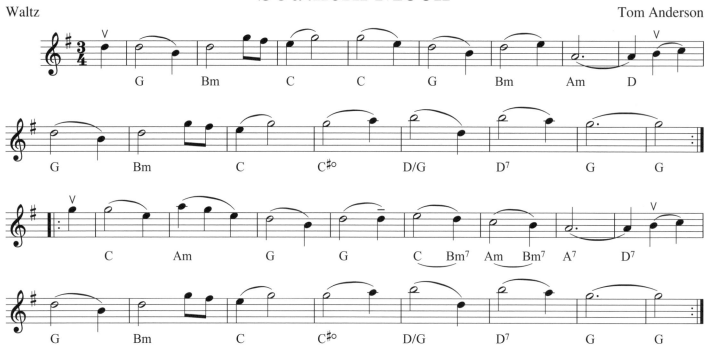

Wilma's Waltz

Waltz

Tom Anderson

HP 31.13

Northern Lights

Waltz

Tom Anderson

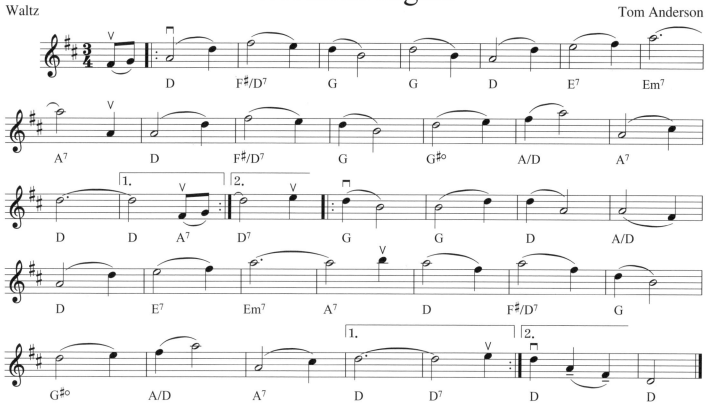

Gossabrough Waltz

Waltz

Tom Anderson

HP 31.13

Mid-Yell School Waltz

Tom Anderson

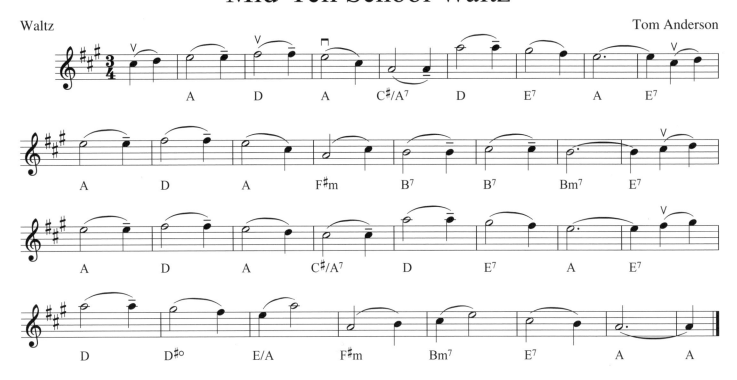

Uyeasoond Bairns

Tom Anderson

HP 31.13

Mr Bill Hardie

Slowish Strathspey

Tom Anderson

© James S. Kerr 1970

Mr John Junner

Reel

Tom Anderson

Laura Malcolmson of Cunningsburgh

Slow Strathspey

Tom Anderson

Reel

Jim Hunter

Strathspey

Tom Anderson

Ness of Braewick

Slow Strathspey

Tom Anderson

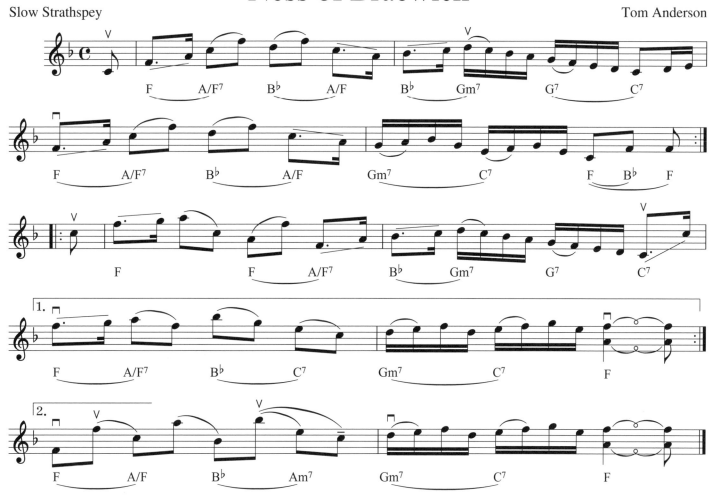

John Fraser of Papa

Strathspey

Tom Anderson

Spey Cottage

Strathspey

Tom Anderson

Twart Dykes

Strathspey

Tom Anderson

HP 31.13

Kirstie's Hornpipe

Hornpipe

Tom Anderson

Rosa's Hornpipe

Hornpipe

Tom Anderson

Skeld Voe Hornpipe

Hornpipe

Tom Anderson

Da Mill Lochs of Ockran

Hornpipe

Tom Anderson

Da Hame Farers

Hornpipe

Tom Anderson

Da Sixereen

Hornpipe

Tom Anderson

Notes on the Music

Avensgarth (p.2). A deserted township on the west side of Hamnavoe, Eshaness, with two crofts and a fishing station. (21/3/72)★

Clyde Valley (p.2). Composed during a visit to Tom's fiddle-playing friend Betty Henderson in Ayr. (5/9/59)

Flangafield (p.3). A prominent hill, east of Murrion, Eshaness.

Lunna Holm (p.3). A little island offshore from Lunna Ness, at the south-east corner of Yell Sound. (4/8/84)

Miss Susan McArthur BEM (p.4). Susan was either a summer school pupil or staff member at Stirling University. (2/7/88)

Mr Bill Paterson (p.4). Bill was a regular attender at the Stirling Summer School. (26/9/87)

Pund Head (p.5). A little headland in Hamnavoe, near Tom's family home.

The Croft of Feal (p.5). Situated near the head of Ronas Voe but now long unoccupied. In times past the Andersons had relatives here. (14/8/83)

Da Auld Resting Chair (p.6). Composed after finding, in his grandfather's derelict house, the remains of the resting chair his grandfather had sat upon when he taught Tom to play the fiddle. (1968)

Daybrak (p. 6). An old Shetland word for dawn. (19/4/85)

Capt. Iain Peterson (p. 7). Son of Laurence Peterson, for whom Tom wrote the lament 'Lowrie o' da Lea'. Iain was a sailor, fiddler, composer and friend. (4/4/91)

Hillswick Wedding (p.8). Tom was playing at dances and weddings while still a teenager. This is an early composition. (1936)

Miss Chris Moffat (p.9). A friend in Ayr, for whom the tune was written during a visit there. (5/9/59)

Da Auld Crü (p.10). The old sheep-pen, usually a communal affair, where all the sheep on a particular grazing or hill would be gathered. (2/7/84)

Dayset (p. 10). An old Shetland word for dusk. (10/6/68)

Ronnie Cooper (p.11). Shetland accordionist, renowned composer and first pianist to Shetland Fiddlers' Society. (1962)

Sands of Braewick (p.11). A stretch of sandy seabed between Eshaness and Hillswick, famous as a haddock fishing ground.

Stenabreck (p.12). A hill-slope west of Braewick, Eshaness. (20/9/84)

The Haa (p.12). The Hall of Tangwick, once home to the local Cheyne landowning family, now restored as a museum. (3/7/85)

Heckie o' da Hulters (p.13). Heckie (Hercules) Johnson was foreman at the Olnafirth whaling station, where Tom worked for a short time. (1982)

Airthrey Castle (p.13). According to Tom "I woke up one morning with this tune running through my head". Airthrey Castle, location of the Stirling Summer Schools, was on the Stirling University campus. (1978)

Angela Hughson's Reel (p.14). Written for a young fiddler from Uyeasound who was one of Tom's first pupils in Unst. (22/5/81)

Backafield (p.14). A small Eshaness croft near the Loch of Braehoulland.

Billy's Tune (p.15). Billy was a Stirling Summer School pupil from Orkney. (2/12/86)

Curly Jamieson (p.15). From Sandness on the south shore of St Magnus Bay, John (Curly) Jamieson was an enthusiastic and devoted member of Shetland Fiddlers' Society. (23/4/84)

Da Blacksmith (p.16). Written for Willie Hunter Senior, a renowned fiddler in his day and father of Willie Hunter Junior. (c.1952)

Da Craig Saet (p.16). A craig saet is a favoured spot on a rocky shore where a fisherman would stand, catching fish with rod and line.

Da Holes o' Scraada (p.17). Formed in the clifftop north of Eshaness lighthouse, by the collapsing of the roof of a large deep sea cave. Originally two holes formed; now there is a single large hole.

Elaine's Reel (p.17). Written for pupil Elaine Tait from Lerwick. (20/5/81)

Gavin Marwick (p.18). A pupil at the Stirling Summer School, now a prominent folk musician. (28/9/82)

Heads of Tingon (p.18). High black cliffs on the coast between Hamnavoe and Ronas Voe. (Nov. 1970)

Hoohivdi (p.19). The nearest house to Moorfield, Tom's birthplace. (27/8/62)

Houlma Sound (p.19). The western exit from Hamnavoe, whose mouth is divided into two channels by a shoal.

Maggie's Reel (p.20). Written for Margaret McKay, of the School of Scottish Studies in Edinburgh. (23/8/69)

Mike Bacchus Reel (p.20). Written for an Irish musicologist friend. (1961)

Miss Lisa Drever (p.21). A young Orcadian pupil at the Stirling Summer School. (18/8/84)

Peerie Twa (p.21). 'Little Two' – written obviously for two children, but there is no record of their identities. (19/11/62)

★ bracketed numbers after the note refer to dates of composition

Pottinger's Reel (p.22). Written for Willie Pottinger of Lerwick, a well-known character and founder-member of Shetland Fiddlers' Society. (5/10/62)

Robertson's Reel (p.22). Written for Davie Robertson, Lerwick accordionist, music shop owner and dance band leader. (1938)

Schiffman's Reel (p.23). Ernst Schiffman, a Swiss, was Church of Scotland missionary in Ollaberry in the 1930s. A competent pianist, he often accompanied Tom and his brothers Bobby and Jamie. (5/12/70)

The Leons (p.23). A prominent hill in Eshaness. (30/9/72)

The Villians of Hamnavoe (p.24). A stretch of fairly flat land along the shore north of Hamnavoe. (21/8/64)

Da Wind ida Claes Line (p.24). The wind in the clothes line! (22/7/74)

Da Laird o' Gulberwick (p.25). Written for Shetland Fiddlers' Society stalwart Andrew Ridland, whose affectionate nickname this was. (c. 1969)

Debbie's Reel (p.25). Written for Debbie Scott, Tom's first female pupil, now a fiddle tutor in Shetland schools. (25/11/77)

Saxavord (p.26). The highest hill on the island of Unst. (1953)

Noup of Noss (p.26). The highest point on the island of Noss. This tune and 'Saxavord' were part of a four-tune reel medley written with Tom Georgeson, to be played for a dance entitled 'The Duke of Edinburgh's Welcome to Shetland'. (1953)

Da Rod ta Houll (p.27). Composed on a visit to Unst; inspired when Tom was walking along the Houll road. (1936)

Da Cannon (p.27). A sea-level cleft in the cliff near Eshaness lighthouse. An explosive noise is created at intervals when big waves roll into it. (13/6/74)

Garderhouse Voe (p.28). Tom's wife Barbara was born at Garderhouse. (c. 1964)

Mavis Grind (p.28). The narrow neck of land near Brae connecting the parish of Northmavine to the mainland of Shetland. (c. 1947)

The Fairy Fiddler (Ruth) (p.29). Ruth was a Stirling Summer School pupil, who always wore red clogs. (2/7/88)

Miss Claire White (p.29). One of Tom's pupils from Lerwick. (29/9/87)

Islesburgh House (p.30). Lerwick's Community and Social Centre for over 50 years. (1947)

Hairst Blinks (p.31). These are a form of sheet lightning, occasionally seen at dusk on fine autumn evenings. (9/5/67)

Miss Jacqueline Young (p.31). Written for a pupil from Lerwick. (21/3/87)

Southern Moon (p.32). The inspiration for this title is unknown.

Wilma's Waltz (p.32). Written for Wilma, wife of Danny Leask, a close friend of Tom's. (4/4/70)

Northern Lights (p.33). *Aurora borealis,* or 'da mirrie dancers' in Shetland. (c. 1950)

Gossabrough Waltz (p.33). Composed at a regatta dance at Yell. (1936)

Mid-Yell School Waltz (p.34). Composed for Tom's pupils there. (c. 1973)

Uyeasoond Bairns (p.34). Composed for Tom's pupils at Uyeasound School in Unst. The alternative spelling of the title reflects the local pronunciation. (1974)

Mr Bill Hardie (p.35). Renowned exponent of the north-east fiddle style and Tom's great friend over many years.

Mr John Junner (p.35). Noted expert on the north-east fiddle tradition; another great friend.

Laura Malcolmson of Cunningsburgh (p.36). A renowned storyteller and authority on Shetland traditions, particularly dances. (27/8/62)

Jim Hunter (p.36). James Hunter's career in broadcasting culminated in his becoming Head of BBC TV Scotland; he now runs his own company, Hunter Productions. Compiler of the anthology *The Fiddle Music of Scotland* (Hardie Press, 1988)

Ness of Braewick (p.37). A low headland on the south coast of Eshaness. (13/9/62)

John Fraser of Papa (p.37). A renowned Papa Stour fiddler and composer. (1949)

Spey Cottage (p.38). The inspiration for this title is unknown.

Twart Dykes (p.38). Simple stone walls enclosing croft boundaries.

Kirstie's Hornpipe (p.39). Written for pupil Kirstie McMillan from Lerwick.

Rosa's Hornpipe (p.39). Rosa was a Stirling Summer School pupil. (30/9/78)

Skeld Voe Hornpipe (p.40). A voe on the west mainland. (13/8/64)

Da Mill Lochs of Ockran (p.40). Little lochs whose waters drove mills at a township north of Hamnavoe. (1955)

Da Hame Farers (p.41). Shetland migrants to all parts of the world who returned *en masse* for a 'hamefarin', the event which led to the founding of Shetland Fiddlers' Society, with Tom as its leader. (1960)

Da Sixereen (p.41). Composed after seeing the remains of one of these six-oared fishing boats. (1947)

Index

	PAGE
Airthrey Castle	13
Angela Hughson's Reel	14
Auld Crü, Da	10
Auld Resting Chair, Da	6
Avensgarth	2
Backafield	14
Billy's Tune	15
Blacksmith, Da	16
Cannon, Da	27
Capt. Iain Peterson	7
Clyde Valley	2
Craig Saet, Da	16
Croft of Feal, The	5
Curly Jamieson	15
Daybrak	6
Dayset	10
Debbie's Reel	25
Elaine's Reel	17
Fairy Fiddler (Ruth), The	29
Flangafield	3
Garderhouse Voe	28
Gavin Marwick	18
Gossabrough Waltz	33
Haa, The	12
Hairst Blinks	31
Hame Farers, Da	41
Heads of Tingon	18
Heckie o' da Hulters	13
Hillswick Wedding	8
Holes o' Scraada, Da	17
Hoohivdi	19
Houlma Sound	19
Islesburgh House	30
Jim Hunter	36
John Fraser of Papa	37
Kirstie's Hornpipe	39
Laird o' Gulberwick, Da	25
Laura Malcolmson of Cunningsburgh	36
Leons, The	23
Lunna Holm	3
Maggie's Reel	20
Mavis Grind	28
Mid-Yell School Waltz	34
Mike Bacchus Reel	20
Mill Lochs of Ockran, Da	40
Miss Chris Moffat	9
Miss Claire White	29
Miss Jacqueline Young	31
Miss Lisa Drever	21
Miss Susan McArthur BEM	4
Mr Bill Hardie	35
Mr Bill Paterson	4
Mr John Junner	35
Ness of Braewick	37
Northern Lights	33
Noup of Noss	26
Peerie Twa	21
Pottinger's Reel	22
Pund Head	5
Rod ta Houll, Da	27
Robertson's Reel	22
Ronnie Cooper	11
Rosa's Hornpipe	39
Sands of Braewick	11
Saxavord	26
Schiffman's Reel	23
Sixereen, Da	41
Skeld Voe Hornpipe	40
Southern Moon	32
Spey Cottage	38
Stenabreck	12
Twart Dykes	38
Uyeasoond Bairns	34
Villians of Hamnavoe, The	24
Wilma's Waltz	32
Wind ida Claes Line, Da	24